Summary of
John Carreyrou's
Bad Blood:
Secrets and Lies in a Silicon Valley Startup
Overview & Analysis by
Summary Genie

Note to readers:

This is an unofficial summary & analysis of John Carreyrou's *Bad Blood: Secrets and Lies in a Silicon Valley Startup* designed to enrich your reading experience. Please buy the original book from Amazon.

Table of Contents

Summary of *Bad Blood* by John Carreyrou

Bad Blood, the bestselling book by Pulitzer Prize-winning reporter, John Carreyrou, is a gripping story of a multibillion-dollar Silicon Valley scam, centered on the biotech startup Theranos and its CEO Elizabeth Holmes and its incredible promise to transform the way blood tests are conducted.

Once considered the female Steve Jobs, this ingenious Stanford dropout was not even twenty years old when she founded Theranos, and soon managed to secure top investors, including Larry Ellison and Tim Draper.

Earning the company a valuation of $9 billion and a near-mythical reputation, her own net worth was estimated at $4.7 billion. The only catch was that the promise upon which this empire was built—that it is possible to run a wide array of medical tests from a single drop of blood—was false.

A gripping work of non-fiction, *Bad Blood* reads like a thriller, yet it is all backed by painstaking research. Carreyrou, the journalist who first broke the story, uses interviews with one hundred fifty subjects, emails, and legal documents to give a detailed account of the biggest corporate fraud since Enron. The only major voice missing is Holmes.' She declined to be interviewed.

Chapter Analysis

Prologue

Carreyrou sets the scene in 2006 when twenty-two-year-old Holmes returns from the company's first major live demonstration for Novartis, a major pharmaceutical company in Switzerland. The presentation is a huge success, and the team is thrilled. Theranos seems the absolute model of an ideal company, with major industry players staffing every part of the company.

There's the chairman of the board, Donald L. Lucas, the venture capitalist, as well as his protégé Larry Ellison. There was a top Stanford Professor, Channing Robertson, as well as a COO with twenty-five years of experience at Pharmaceutical and biotechnology companies, Diane Parks. The senior vice president, John Howard, came from Panasonic.

Even more exciting was the attention the company had been getting from pharmaceutical companies, who promised to make it a lucrative endeavor. The only tiny discomfort felt by Henry Mosley, Theranos' chief financial officer, was that Holmes had asked him to revise his financial projections for investors, to make them even more appealing. Still, the request didn't seem to go beyond the reasonable, and he did it.

Mosley also wasn't sure he knew how the Theranos technology worked, but that wasn't his area of expertise; he just had to take care of the finances. He had watched demos by Shaunok Roy, Theranos' cofounder who had a Ph.D. in chemical engineering from Stanford. In the demo, Roy would prick his finger and squeeze a few drops of blood onto a small white credit-card-sized cartridge and then put it into a box the size of a toaster known as a reader that would extract data and beam it to a server that would then beam back the result.

After Holmes' Switzerland trip, Mosley noticed a strange attitude in the rest of the team, compared to her exuberant positivity. He spoke to Roy who eventually admitted why the team was so glum: because the technology was unreliable, they often resorted to using fake, pre-recorded results in order to ensure success. Mosley knew they had crossed the line. He confronted the charismatic Holmes that very afternoon.

At the meeting, where they were to discuss continued successes, including an increase in the company's valuation, Mosley brought up what he had heard. At first, she deflected his concerns but when he insisted, she turned icy and fired him on the spot.

A daughter of illustrious and successful parents, Holmes showed an inventive spirit at a young age—as well as a competitive nature. She wanted to be both incredibly rich and also "purposeful," a value that she got from her upbringing.

Stanford was the natural destination of this straight-A student, who already had ties to the school thanks to the years her family spent living there when she was a girl. It was then, in the late 1980s, that she befriended a girl named Jesse Draper, the daughter of Tim Draper, a venture capitalist who would one day help Theranos get its start.

At Stanford Holmes met Channing Robertson, who let her work in his lab after she took his Chemical Engineering class—forging another relationship that would be essential to Theranos' success. By the end of her freshman year, she was already planning to start a company.

Then, in the summer after her sophomore year, a summer internship at the Genome Institute of Singapore testing patient specimens with low-tech methods inspired her to find a better way. In a mad rush of only five days, she used what she had learned from Dr. Robertson's class and her experience in Singapore to draft a patent application for an arm patch able to diagnose and treat medical conditions.

She and her Stanford colleague Shaunak opened an office in a dangerous part of Menlo Park and began raising money from Tim Draper, the father of her childhood friend. More than just $1 million, the money gave Holmes credibility thanks to Draper's family reputation in Silicon

Valley. With brightly colored documents and a peppy sales pitch, she was able to raise $6 million by the end of 2004.

As they developed the device, they needed to make compromises, as her original idea of a hand-held device similar to a glucose monitor, was proving to be impossible. They compromised by developing a cartridge-and-reader system that became the first prototype, developed in 2005. They also had two dozen employees and an ambitious business model that promised to quickly generate revenues. By Christmas of that year, Holmes was already referring to Theranos as the "hottest start-up in the Valley."

In 2006, Edmond Ku was brought aboard Theranos to help engineer a working prototype for Theranos. However, he faced numerous constraints, stemming from the fact that Holmes was fixated on the need to use an extremely small quantity of blood for testing. This, coupled with her insistence on making the device small as well, created more engineering challenges than Ku had ever experienced.

The materials they used for testing, single-use cartridges that were extremely costly meant that they were burning through their startup money. With $6 million already gone, they underwent a second round of fundraising that got them another $9 million.

Furthermore, Ku had to work with a group of biochemists, with whom he had a poor working relationship, worsened by Holmes' insistence that they seldom communicate. By keeping the information compartmentalized, only she had an understanding of how the system was developing.

In the face of difficulties, Holmes only accelerated their working speed, pushing Ku to do more, even as the company was experiencing high rates of turn-over. She seemed disinterested in preserving the staff, insisting instead that people were interchangeable and only the company mattered.

The only people who seemed to be able to influence Holmes was an older Pakistani man named Sunny, and Silicon Valley investors Don Lucas and Larry Ellison. Ellison, one of the richest people in the world, had a reputation for bending the truth from his years at Oracle.

At the same time, Holmes created a rival engineering team and put Ku under pressure: they had to be ready for a pilot project with Pfizer to test units in people's homes in Tennessee. In August 2007 as the company grew to seventy employees, they began the test, and Ku only felt more anxious when he learned the test involved terminal cancer patients. Holmes, instead, was excited.

Competition between the engineering teams intensified while the mood at the company was tense: Holmes and Theranos were filling a lawsuit against former employees for stealing information. Ku's competition was an Irishman named Tony Nugent, known for his no-nonsense attitude. Together with the help of another engineer named Dave Nelson, Nugent bought a robot made for dispensing glue.

By September 2007, they were able to make a prototype for a smaller version that would be the mechanism used for testing blood—and it only required 50 microliters, basically a drop. This "gluebot" was highly sophisticated, and used a longstanding technique called chemiluminescent immunoassay.

Suddenly, Theranos had its way forward, and Nelson and Nugent seemed to have won the competition against Ku who was fired a few weeks before Thanksgiving. In order to get his severance, he had to sign a non-disclosure and non-disparagement agreement. Shaunak followed Ku and resigned two weeks later, disappointed that the "gluebot" was the not-so-exciting technology that was meant to lead the company forward. He and Holmes parted on good terms.

Although Nelson "won" the competition, he was also feeling uncomfortable. He had barely put the prototype together and tested its basic safety and Holmes was already taking it out of the office for demonstrations.

In 2007, Holmes, was effected by a strong case of "apple envy," and even called her device "the iPod of health care." She began recruiting Apple employees, including Ana Arriola, who became the chief design architect at Theranos. Arriola not only designed a fashionable look for the device, but she also gave Elizabeth a makeover, upgrading her sweats to a more Steve Jobs look of a black turtleneck and black slacks.

Still, Arriola and her fellow new hires notice a number of quirks, including the IT department's prohibition of messaging with coworkers by blocking chat ports – intended to protect intellectual property but actually causing them to lose hours of productivity. They also felt spied upon, and people were constantly getting fired (like Ed Ku and twenty others).

When Arriola finally got to spend time talking to some engineers outside of the office, she learned about the possibly unethical elements of the Tennessee study, which was using an untested device and which would not be used to actually improve the subjects' treatment—but only to test the effectiveness of Theranos' device. None of this had been explained to the employees.

Arriola reached out to a former Apple colleague, Avie Tevanian, a close friend of Steve Jobs and a member of Theranos' board of directors. He confided in her that he, too, was having doubts of his own. Tevanian had had a great first impression of Holmes who was enthusiastic and very receptive to his advice in their first meeting.

However, after a few board meetings, Tevanian began to notice a pattern: revenues promised but never realized, contracts unavailable for viewing, and repeated delays for the project's rollout—with shifting stories about why the delay. When Holmes took steps to create foundation for tax-planning purposes, which would significantly increase her power, Tevanian began to push back to the board chairman, Don Lucas. Lucas, who doted on Holmes, was not responsive and told Tevanian he should consider resigning.

Tevanian then went and reviewed the documents in his possession and realized that within a single year, the entire company had changed, including the executive team. He planned to show Lucas what he uncovered. The two met in person and Lucas simply encouraged Tevanian to resign. Lucas' only concerns were that Tevanian hand over the questionable documents to him and that he waive his rights to buy additional stocks in the company. Soon after, this was followed by a letter threatening a lawsuit. Tevanian, whose personal wealth was rather secure, decided to walk away.

Arriola was also getting increasingly nervous at this time, especially when Tevanian told her that Lucas and Holmes wanted to push him off the board. Her relationship with Holmes had also been getting worse: Holmes was secretive, a quality that made Arriola's designer job more difficult. When she brought her engineering concerns about the Tennessee study to Holmes, she was shut-down. Holmes implied she should resign, and Arriola decided that was the right course of action. She resigned that day.

By early 2008, Theranos had a fancy new address, a significant improvement in status for the company that stressed out those who were tasked with making it happen, including IT head Matt Bissel. Holmes pushed him too far during the move, forcing him to try to save a month's rent by rushing the process in an aggressive way, an event that became the breaking point for Bissel. He had already seen Holmes' bad behavior, the way she crushed dissent, fired people left and right, and even collected a dossier of damaging information to use against them as leverage if needed. He left that month.

Just as the new, smaller Theranos was getting settled into its posh, too big office, the engineers left behind by Arriola—Aaron Moore, Justin Maxwell and Mike Bauerly—started getting nervous too. They had started to do some user testing with the "gluebots," and the tests went poorly. It took way more than one attempt to get enough blood for a healthy, young person, which means an older or less healthy patient would have an even harder time.

To blow off steam, Moore made a fake craigslist ad pretending to sell the device. When he brought it to work, his colleagues laughed, but Holmes—who thought it was real—was furious and set about investigating the perpetrator. Moore confessed, but his reputation with Holmes was permanently damaged. He lost his chance to move to the sales department.

Fortunately for Moore, sales was not the place to be at the time. Sales had just gotten a new head, a sales executive named Todd Surdey. When he came on board, he started talking to sales subordinates based on the East

Coast, including Susan DiGiaimo, who admitted that the revenue forecasts were vastly overinflated.

Theranos would have to prove its functionality to each of its partners, as it attempted to do in the 2007 Tennessee study with Pfizer, or risk losing the contract. DiGiaimo also admitted she had never seen any data to back up Holmes' claims and often witnessed device malfunctioning when she went with Holmes on demonstrations, like the Novartis trip. Surdey took his concern to the general counsel, a man named Michael Esquivel who had concerns of his own.

From there, in March 2008, the two went to speak to a board member, Tom Brodeen, an experienced business man in his mid-sixties. He was relatively new to the board and told them to go straight to Lucas, the chairman, who took their concerns seriously because of Surdey's stature.

After calling an emergency meeting of the board without Holmes, they decided to remove Holmes as CEO. Yet within two hours of receiving the news, Holmes convinced them to let her try again, promising to mend her ways. One of her first acts was to fire both Surdey and Esquivel, leaving the engineers (Moore, Bauerly and Maxwell) all the more wary.

Maxwell quit soon after, and Moore and Bauerly stayed only a few more months. No one who remained seemed willing to tell Holmes that she needed to slow down in her frenetic push to sell a product that was not yet ready.

Holmes' work at Theranos attracted the attention of Richard Fuisz, an old family acquaintance with an entrepreneurial background and a huge ego and a lifestyle to match. He had a history of carrying out vendettas against those who crossed him, and felt slighted that no one in the Holmes family had sought out his advice on this new venture, considering his elevated stature. Still, he was curious and opportunistic and sought to get involved.

Listening to an NPR interview, he spotted a weak point in the technology and thought he could patent it—and then sell it to Theranos or someone else: a mechanism in the device that alerted a doctor if the patient's results came back abnormal.

Over the months in which he worked on the patent, combining several existing technologies into one, the Holmes family had no idea what he was up to – even though they continued to socialize. Only in January 2008 was it available on an official online database, and only five months after that did Theranos find it.

Holmes' father, Chris, set out to do something about Fuisz's theft of his daughter's idea, so he visited his friend Chuck Work who agreed to see Elizabeth and advise her on a potential lawsuit. Eventually he declined to take her case and thought that was the end of the story with Theranos.

Holmes invited her Stanford best friend, Chelsea Burkett to join her at Theranos in the client solutions group, the group in charge of setting up the validation studies to win clients. Her first assignment was with Johnson & Johnson. Another old friend joined the team, Ramesh "Sunny" Balwani, who had a vague title and romantic ties to Holmes from back when she studied in Beijing.

Sunny was aggressive and powerful, and frequently dismissive and demeaning to employees. He had already had tax troubles and embraced an affluent lifestyle. His presence set things off on a rocky path for Burkett, who didn't even know if he was her boss or she was his. His job was to write code, but his boasts never seemed to add up. It was also unclear whether he and Holmes were still romantically involved. She claimed they weren't, but later that would prove false.

When Burkett traveled to Belgium in fall 2009 for her first assignment, she went with Daniel Young, a bioengineer from MIT. The two faced challenges because the machines were still not functioning reliably. In order to use such a small amount of blood, the blood had to be diluted. But if it got too diluted, the results wouldn't be accurate. The ambient temperature had to be precisely 34 degrees Celsius, which was a challenge in colder settings like certain hospitals.

Sunny always dismissed such concerns and blamed poor cellular connection. At the same time that Burkett was having her troubles, Theranos also received word that Pzfizer was ending their partnership because of underwhelming results from Tennessee.

Her next trip was to Mexico where the Swine Flu provided what Holmes hoped would be an ideal setting to market Theranos. Here things went just as badly, and scientists within the company were discouraging about the logic of testing Swine Flu (usually tested by nasal swab) by blood.

Sunny also traveled to Thailand where gossip was emerging about his unethical methods of collecting samples. Burkett started getting scared, all the more so as firing continued in 2009 and 2010, a job left to Sunny. Employes referred to it as "Sunny disappearing someone." After only six months on the job, by February 2010, Burkett was ready to quit. Then she learned that the company had been encouraging patients to use their untested devices to make medical decisions, and she decided it was time to go.

In 2010, Theranos began discussions with Walgreens and got involved with Dr. J, Jay Rosen, a doctor who worked for big corporations and was a member of Walgreens' innovation team. He was joined by Kevin Hunter, who met with Holmes and Sunny.

The teams hit it off and Walgreens was speeding into the relationship. Yet Hunter was suspicious when Holmes didn't let him see the lab and couldn't talk confidently about different kinds of blood tests. He also was bothered by Sunny. Still, Dr. J was convinced by them, so they went ahead.

Part way through negotiations, Theranos changed what it was offering Walgreens, another red flag for Hunter. He took his concerns up the chain, but his superiors feared losing the technology to CVS, their competitor. Hunter kept at it, and eventually was able to debunk the "study" that Theranos used to claim the device's validity. However, Walgreens' management changed and Hunter's efforts failed. Safeway also signed on with Theranos, and new in-store labs were being planned.

With Walgreens and Safeway on board, Theranos had to develop a machine with a lot more capabilities, so Holmes hired Kent Frankovich and Greg Baney, as engineers. Tasked with developing a minilab, Frankovich and Baney had to miniaturize and combine many existing technologies, with Homes insisting that they immediately develop the prototype in the small scale she wanted, rather than develop first, shrink later, as they preferred.

Becoming close to Holmes, Baney began to have some suspicions about her, especially when he found out that she was romantically involved with Sunny and hadn't disclosed it to anyone.

In 2011, Holmes hired her younger brother Christian, despite his lack of credentials, who then hired four of his friends from Duke and then a fifth, known as the Frat Pack. Baney's sister eventually applied to the company, too, in April, but when she declined it, Baney's honeymoon with the company ended.

Kent had his own troubles with the company, when he created a successful kickstarter on a bike light he had created and Holmes demanded he surrender the patent to Theranos. They agreed, instead, to let him take a leave of absence, further straining Baney's workload. He left at the end of his first year there, once his stock had vested.

After many delays, in 2012 the partnership with Safeway was starting to come to fruition, which would be crucial to bolster the sagging fortunes of the grocery chain. Theranos took over the blood testing at an employee health clinic on its corporate campus. Yet their methods did not match their claims, as they were actually using traditional phlebotomists to draw blood from people's arms as well as doing the finger-prick. Nor did they test onsite but send the blood to a lab in Palo Alto, staffed by inexperienced personnel.

Employee test results also started coming back with strange abnormalities—and it turned out that the phlebotomists in the employee clinic were also untrained in the methods they needed to use. Diana Dupuy, the employee who realized the shortcomings and brought them to the company's attention, was also fired, and the relationship with Safeway continued on through 2012 and 2013.

As the launch date for the actual wellness centers kept getting pushed back, the executives got angry and eventually pushed out the CEO who had started the project with Theranos.

In 2011, Theranos planned to get its devices adopted by the military in the Afghan war, but Holmes ran up against Lieutenant Colonel David Shoemaker, who was not convinced by her testing plans which would avoid the FDA. This was a dealbreaker for him, but a year later, Theranos insisted again which earned them a surprise visit from a CMS (Centers for Medicare and Medicate Services) investigator, putting Holmes into attack mode.

Still, the company was given a chance to do blood tests on leftover samples of blood that were no longer needed to inform the treatment of wounded soldiers, which seemed like a fair opportunity and compromise. Nonetheless, they did not take advantage of it, even into mid-2013.

The story jumps back to 2011, as Theranos serves a lawsuit against Fuisz over the patent he developed, with a high-powered attorney to represent them: David Boies. The lawsuit stretched out over months and began becoming extremely costly, yet there was one positive development.

Fuisz noticed that there was a co-inventor listed on Holmes' patents, Ian Gibbons, a Ph.D. in biochemistry with about fifty patents to his name. He planned to interview him to see if they could use him to debunk Holmes' claims that Fuisz had stolen from her.

Ian Gibbons joined Theranos in 2005 and worked there for five years, as a specialist in immunoassays. Passionate about blood science, he was skeptical of Holmes' leadership style and during the Walgreens courtship, eventually got fed up and was soon fired. Then Sunny agreed to demote him to an in-house consultant, so he continued on but was severally demoralized.

By 2013, when he was subpoenaed to testify in the Fuisz trial, Gibbons was wrestling with a deep clinical depression. His drinking intensified as he faced testifying, and his wife realized he was in need of professional help. On May 16, she found him at home unresponsive and he died a week later, with enough painkillers in his system to kill a horse.

Theranos hired portrait photographer Martin Schoeller as part of a secret marketing campaign run by TBWA\Chiat\Day, the agency that had represented Apple. The move to hire such a high profile firm, costing $6 million per year, was unusual for a startup.

She made demands of her new agency that they make bold claims on the website, boasting Theranos' accuracy and abilities, that were not actually true. She refused to show corroborating studies to the firm, which made her collaborators suspicious—and worried about their own legal liability in promoting false medical claims.

The launch of the website was fraught with chaos, including a breakdown on the part of Holmes. While two employees of Chiat\Day were suspicious, their higher-ups dismissed them, saying that all startups are chaotic and secretive.

Alan Beam was a South African pathologist who got started at Theranos a few weeks before the launch in 2013 when morale was low thanks to a dysfunctional corporate culture. Sunny was elevating sycophants to key positions, despite actual industry experience. Holmes was demanding that the miniLab do more and more things while staying the same tiny size.

Under pressure to meet the Walgreens contract by February 2013, while everything was going haywire, Holmes and Sunny decided to make it happen by cheating. Beam finally saw a crack in Holmes' façade as she shakily assured him they would make it to launch the project, promising she had a fallback in mind.

Another chemist, Anjali Laghari, was also feeling unsettled that the company continued to relax its standards in pursuit of the launch. She too resigned. The atmosphere got more tense, with Holmes announcing to the remaining employees that she was building a religion.

In September 2013, as Theranos and Holmes were being celebrated in the *Wall Street Journal,* top investors were being invited to invest up to $15 million in Theranos. She got huge Silicon Valley names and money started pouring into the company.

Theranos was becoming a "unicorn," a startup valued at $1 billion or more. Two hedge fund managers, Christopher James and Brian Grossman got interested, and they were won over by its board of directors and a pitch from Sunny and Holmes that listed bold claims about Theranos' revolutionary capabilities.

Thanks to the pedigree of the board, they never considered that the company's internal projections were five to twelve times lower than the ones they had been shown. Thanks to their investment, the company was worth $9 billion with Holmes' net worth at almost $5 billion.

Tyler Shultz—grandson of George, former Secretary of State—started working at Theranos right as the Walgreens technology was going live, and he befriended another new hire named Erika Cheung. Despite the chaos, he was inspired by Holmes' vision, but as soon as he saw a quick demo of the rudimentary technology, he was immediately depressed. He and Cheung learned about techniques to falsify data in order to get tests approved.

Meanwhile, Alan Beam was also encountering problems with potassium testing. Beam went behind Sunny and Holmes' back to conduct his own tests, to verify that the official results had been falsified, infuriating them. Shultz brought the news to his grandfather, who suggested he bring the concerns to Sunny and Holmes, which eventually elicited and aggressive response from Sunny, belittling all Shultz's knowledge. He decided to resign, against the advice of his powerful family and under the shadow of retribution. Cheung decided to follow him soon after.

Jumping back to the Fuisz lawsuit, the death of Ian Gibbons had been a major setback. They had already spent $2 million on their defense, so they decided to settle. Bitter about the supposed resolution, Richard's son John emailed a reporter named Julia Love and began to tell her their story, which resulted in an article in Litigation Daily.

The article came to the attention of Roger Parloff of *Fortune Magazine* who started making inquiries into the case and eventually flew to Palo Alto to interview Holmes. Holmes promised him a scoop and used the opportunity to talk up her new ventures. The journalist didn't even reach out to the Fuisz's to hear their side of the story.

Parloff's June 2014 cover story made Holmes an instant star. In September she captivated a crowd at a TEDMED conference, where she told an exaggerated story about her uncle's tragic death and how it inspired her. Theranos planned another move to accommodate its growing work force, and the Chiat\Day firm was becoming increasingly enmeshed in their design and marketing. A documentary filmmaker was brought on board to film spots with Holmes as the star.

By October 2014, Holmes was Silicon Valley royalty, but Alan Beam was reaching his breaking point when he realized that Theranos' cheating on the test results was breaking the law and began to share his concerns and plan his resignation.

After he left, he was harassed by company lawyers, and the lawyer he hired to protect himself gave into the pressure. Under her advice, he signed an affidavit for the company and deleted one hundred seventy-five emails.

Around this time, a profile on Holmes was published in the *New Yorker* and was starting to attract some skepticism from the scientific community, particularly in regards to the unknown scientific journals substantiating Holmes' claims.

A blogger named Adam Clapper wrote a post enumerating his question marks, and soon Richard Fuisz discovered the post and they began to work together. Soon, Fuisz also discovered Alan Beam via Linkedin, and let Clapper know about this new source. Clapper then brought the story to *Bad Blood's* author, John Carreyrou at the *Wall Street Journal,* thanks to his reputation for reporting on lab-industry abuses.

Clapper shared his concerns with Carreyrou, who had also noticed holes in the *New Yorker* story, such as lack of peer-reviewed data. Carreyrou began his investigation, talking to the Fuisz's as well as Rochelle Gibbons, Ian's widow, who relayed her dead husband's suspicions that the Theranos machines did not work.

These conversations led him to Alan Beam, his first major source. He laid out the entire story for Carreyrou, about the manipulation of the blood tests and all the cover-ups inside the company. Still, with only one anonymous source, Carreyrou could not yet go on the record, especially after he learned that Beam had deleted his emails on his lawyer's advice. Eventually he was able to get in contact with twenty current or former Theranos employees, but was still lacking an open source until Tyler Shultz came forward.

Now Carreyrou was ready to do some tests of his own to confirm the inaccuracy of the Theranos machines. He enlisted the help of Nicole Sundene, an Arizona doctor, who ordered identical blood tests from two different labs, giving him his first independent evidence. Then he was able to build on his story by interviewing Erika Cheung and Rochelle Gibbons. Holmes, however, refused to be interviewed.

When Theranos discovered Tyler Shultz's cooperation with Carreyrou, they began pressuring his family who in turn pressured him, sending lawyers to threaten him. Tyler held firm, denied the allegations and refused to sign anything from Theranos despite escalating threats from the company to bankrupt his entire family.

Meanwhile, Carreyrou was trying to secure an interview with Holmes who was happily doing the talk show circuit. He only managed to get an interview with a Theranos representative, Daniel Young, and they agreed to visit the office of the *Wall Street Journal* for the meeting.

The meeting with Theranos' legal team and Daniel Young in June 2015 felt like the prelude to a legal proceeding. They put pressure on him to divulge his sources and insisted they would debunk any claim Carreyrou had of a story of fraud. They refused to give him any information about Theranos' trade secrets unless they all signed non-disclosure agreements.

At the same time, Theranos was making threats against Erika Chang and Alan Beam, suspecting them of being sources and violating their affidavits. Even Dr. Sundene was being threatened, as were other doctors who had agreed to help. Carreyrou was starting to lose some of his sources as the pressure mounted.

In July 2015, Theranos was getting ready to enjoy some positive news, including the passage of a law in Arizona that would allow patients to bypass doctors and test their blood independently. Joe Biden was planning a visit to the lab, and they had placed a dermatologist as a nominal figure head to replace Alan Beam and created a fake laboratory to impress the vice president.

They even published an op-ed in the *Journal* in order to celebrate their successes and encourage others to follow in their footsteps. Still, other negatives kept cropping up, like devastatingly bad reviews on Glassdoor that revealed the unethical behavior of the company and dizzyingly high turnover amongst the staff.

Carreyrou started to put pressure on his editor to put out the story as soon as possible, who cautioned a more strategic approach that mimicked *la mattanza,* a Sicilian fishing ritual in which fishermen waited for hours until they were in the perfect position to strike their prey. They planned to launch the story in October right before a major planned appearance of Holmes'.

Holmes had just secured $125 million from Rubert Murdoch, owner of the *Journal,* the biggest investment he had ever made outside his media assets. She tried to use their relationship to get him to quash Carreyrou's story, but he declined to intervene and allowed it to go forward.

The lawyers also tried their own tactics, including offering the *Journal* a demonstration, but Carreyrou and his team were unwilling to accept their wishy-washy promises. The story was published on October 15, 2015 with an understated headline and a devastating series of revelations.

It stirred up a huge response, much of it supportive but much of it disbelieving, and Holmes went on counter-attack going on TV and playing the part of the Silicon Valley visionary. She discredited the *Journal,* and the former employees, calling them "confused," and put out a lengthy rebuttal on her website.

Theranos changed its board of directors, removing Shultz and others and replacing them with their lawyer, David Boies, who threatened the possibility of a defamation lawsuit against the *Journal.* As Carreyrou continued to publish a series of articles detailing the weaknesses of Theranos, he looked to regulatory agencies for support, knowing that he needed them to take action against the company for any of this to have any meaning.

Ultimately it was Erika Cheung's email complaint to the CMS that sparked the needed inspection of the Theranos laboratory. In January 2016, Carreyrou obtained the results of the inspection that revealed serious deficiencies in the Newark lab that posed dangers to patient health and threatened their federal certification—a major blow.

In response, Holmes blamed Sunny, breaking up with him and firing him as a fall guy. Still, they were hit with a ban from the CMS prohibiting Holmes and her company from the lab business. She nonetheless wanted one more chance to wow the world with her technology and planned a display for August of that year – a virtuoso performance but one that was still lacking substance.

Other publications followed up on the *Journal*'s reporting. Her fancy legal team and she parted ways after a disagreement. Holmes failed to appeal the CMS ban and closed the company's labs. The state of Arizona forced them to settle for $4.65 million to cover the blood tests of 76,217 Arizonans.

Epilogue

Ultimately this story of hubris, fraud and collapse comes down to one person: Elizabeth Holmes. A talented, charismatic leader (and possible sociopath), Holmes was able to develop a vision into a reality by convincing countless other people to believe in her. She believed so deeply in her vision and was so determined to reach it, that she didn't care who or what she jeopardized. Eventually all the hype crashed into reality, leaving Theranos an empty shell of its creator's dream.

Background Information about *Bad Blood*

Bad Blood has been named one of the best books of 2018 by a number of prestigious outlets, including *The Washington Post, The New York Times* and National Public Radio. It was named the McKinsey Business Book of the Year and an Amazon Top Ten Book of the Month Pick.

According to Molly Brown at geekwire.com, "It's a page-turner filled with office politics, power struggles, corruption, abuse, on and on, making this book a must-read and a cautionary tale of what not to do for startups."

Bad Blood received accolades from important figures in tech, including Microsoft visionary Bill Gates, who enthused: "The story is even crazier than I expected, and I found myself unable to put it down once I started. This book has everything: elaborate scams, corporate intrigue, magazine cover stories, ruined family relationships, and the demise of a company once valued at nearly $10 billion." A film version, starring Jennifer Lawrence and directed by Adam McKay, is currently in the works. There is no firm release date, but it is projected for 2020.

Background Information about John Carreyrou

Author John Carreyrou, a French-American journalist, is a member of the Wall Street Journal's investigative reporting team. Educated at Duke University, he has been based in Brussels, Paris and New York City where he currently lives. His reporting on Theranos began in 2014. After reading a profile in the *New Yorker* he became curious about Holmes' meteoric rise. He had already two Pulitzers to his name and an expertise in whistle-blowing, when he began his research into Theranos.

Although he faced threats of lawsuits from Holmes, thanks to Carreyrou's reporting, Theranos' massive fraud was revealed, and Holmes and Sunny are currently under indictment. As of June 2018, despite the possibility that she might spend up to ten years behind bars, Carreyrou reported that Holmes was shopping around for new investors for an entirely new start-up venture.

Trivia Questions about *Bad Blood*

1. What lucky connections to Silicon Valley helped Holmes get her start?

2. Who were Holmes' early confidants?

3. What was the "gluebot"?

4. What problems started when Walgreens and Safeway signed on as retail partners?

5. What role did the design firm Chiat\Day have in Theranos' success?

6. How did the media contribute to Holmes' rise to fame?

Discussion Questions for *Bad Blood*

1. To what do you attribute Holmes' success?

2. What were the biggest mistakes Holmes' made during the early days of Theranos?

3. Who do you think was best positioned to stop the scam and why?

4. Do you think Holmes deserves to go to prison? Why or why not?

5. Do you think the Theranos debacle will be a setback for biotech startups?

6. How would you compare the Theranos fraud to other massive industry frauds, such as Enron?

7. Do you think Holmes is a sociopath? How do you explain her behavior?

Thank You!

We hope you've enjoyed your reading experience. Our team at Summary Genie is constantly striving to deliver to you the highest quality summary guides. We'd like to thank you for supporting us and reading until the very end.

Before you go, would you kindly please leave us a review on Amazon? It would mean a lot to us and it will support our work in creating more high quality summary guides for you in the future.

Thank you once again!

Warmly yours,

The Summary Genie Team

Made in the USA
Middletown, DE
28 May 2019